CLEANS

FOR BODY & SPIRIT

Anne Charlish

Haldane Mason

First published in the UK in 2000 by
Haldane Mason Ltd
59 Chepstow Road
London W2 5BP

Reprinted 2001, 2002

ISBN: 1-902463-58-7 (hbk)
ISBN: 1-902463-62-5 (pbk)

A HALDANE MASON BOOK

Editors: Jean Coppendale, Ali Glenny, Beck Ward
Design: Louise Millar

Colour reproduction by CK Digital Ltd, UK

Printed in UAE

Picture Acknowledgements
Sue Ford: 9, 11, 19, 24, 25b, 43, 57, 59, 62; **Amanda Heywood:** 13, 23; **Andrew Sydenham:** 1, 4,
7, 15, 17, 20, 31, 35, 37, 39, 45, 49, 51, 55, 57, 58; **Image Bank:** /Marc Romanelli: 41;
/White/Packert: 23; /Kaz Mori: 25; /L.D. Gordon: 28; **Tony Stone Images:** 29

Contents

Introduction

The benefits of cleansing, in whatever form, are now well recognized for those who wish to improve their health, raise their energy levels, and fight off chronic fatigue and common minor disorders such as headache, backache, mouth ulcers, irritable bowel syndrome, eczema, allergy and asthma. This book is filled with suggestions to help you to tone up all the systems of your body, including the digestive system, the respiratory system, the cardiovascular system, the brain and nervous system and the muscles.

In the increasingly fast-paced world of the twenty-first century, we need all the means at our disposal to make the very most of our busy lives. It is all too easy to neglect our health or personal fulfilment and thus fail to achieve our real potential.

We fill our bodies with toxins on a daily basis, without even thinking about it.

We are surrounded everywhere, every day, by toxins and pollutants in many forms. It is not practical to avoid most of these. How can we avoid traffic, for example, or electricity pylons? But some toxins – such as tobacco smoke, alcohol and caffeine – are avoidable.

WATER – THE BEST DRINK IN THE WORLD

There is a lot that we can do to help improve our own immune systems. Cleansing and detoxing programmes offer us some of the best ways of invigorating and refreshing both body and soul. One of the foundation stones of healthy living and a body that functions well is ensuring our daily intake of water. We all need at least 1.5 litres (2.5 pints) of water every day, not counting tea or coffee. In fact, a large caffeine intake means that we will need to drink more water every day in order to flush out the caffeine. Water will help to prevent dehydration, headache, tension, swelling of the ankles, bloatedness of the stomach, as well as improving the overall quality of the skin. You may imagine that this intake of liquid would be impossible – but after a few days our bodies become accustomed to it and like it. This is one of the most important messages of this book: not only does cleansing have valuable benefits, but it is enjoyable, too.

Ideal healthy living and quality of life also has to include the right balance of diet and a certain amount of exercise. We all have to get these right for our physical and emotional health – they are another absolute bedrock of cleansing.

Cleansing doesn't just work on the inside, however; cleansing the physical body using treatments and techniques will help to improve our sense of well-being, both physically and spiritually. And talking of spirituality, mind cleansing is possibly one of the most forgotten aspects of cleansing and caring for the body. It is well known that unhappiness and stress affect not only the mind but also the body, therefore the techniques described here will also assist in the physical detoxification processes.

Nothing suggested in this book is excessively prescriptive or detailed, because most of us have to incorporate our cleansing processes into our normal everyday lives. Your cleansing will be no less beneficial and revitalizing for that. Indeed, your programme may become a potent tool in learning new health habits that stay with you for good.

This book has been planned to provide you with plenty of practical suggestions and ideas to help you to achieve a cleaner, calmer attitude to improving your quality of life.

Food

AND

What we eat and drink each day plays an invaluable part in cleansing our system and refreshing both body and mind. This section includes some easy to follow ideas and suggestions for a healthy diet.

Aim to eat something each day from each of the four main food groups and you will reap the benefits ten-fold; stopping smoking is also especially helpful when cleansing. And why not think about revitalizing your immune system – it may be easier and more fun than you think. Remember the following:

● food nourishes us and gives us energy, keeping our bodies working
● some of the foods we eat are vital for internal cleansing of the body

Diet

You are what you eat

Yes, what they say is true. Eating healthily and well, at regular intervals and not too close to bedtime, really pays rich dividends in how your body and mind function.

Fibre, in the form of vegetables and grains, for example, is invaluable in cleansing the body. Too much protein and fat clogs the arteries, slows down the system and makes us feel sluggish after eating.

HOW DO YOU FEEL?

Look in the mirror; what do you see? Assess your body tone and the condition of your skin and hair. These are vital pointers as to how well you are eating. Treat your body like a temple. Don't insult it with junk. Like any engine, your body runs best on top quality fuel.

ARE YOU ROUGHLY THE RIGHT WEIGHT?

Check your Body Mass Index (BMI) in preference to simply looking at your weight. This is how you work out your BMI:

1 If you weigh yourself in pounds, convert it to kilograms by dividing your weight in pounds by 2.2
2 Convert your height to metres by working out your height in inches and dividing the result by 39.4. Then square the resulting number
3 Now divide your weight in kilograms (1) by your height in metres (2); this is your BMI

For example:
1 143lbs = 65 kg (your weight)
2 65 in = 1.65 m (your height); 1.65 × 1.65 = 2.72
3 65 ÷ 2.72 = 24
Your BMI is 24

A BMI of over 40 is a serious health risk. The ideal is between 20 and 25. If your BMI is over 30, ideally you need to cleanse with a detox programme and try to lose some weight. If your BMI is under 20, you should concentrate on eliminating harmful toxins and gaining weight through eating protein and carbohydrate.

Taking five or ten minutes for breakfast really will boost your brain power first thing in the morning.

WHAT YOU NEED

You should try to eat something from each of the following four main food groups every day:

1 protein from meat, poultry or fish
2 protein and calcium from dairy products such as eggs, cheese, milk and milk products
3 protein from nuts, peas, beans, lentils, soya and pulses
4 carbohydrates and fibre from pulses and grains and, to a lesser extent, from fruit and vegetables

Eat one of the following at least once a day for optimum cleansing and detoxing: wholewheat cereal, wholemeal foods such as bread, pasta or savoury biscuits without added sugar. Add to this as many salads and vegetables as you can eat.

You also need to drink at least eight glasses of water every day. Try to start the day by drinking a glass of water with a squeeze of fresh lemon juice for ultra inner cleansing.

The role of diet

There are 500 million bacteria in one average gut, or, to give it its proper name, gastrointestinal system. All these bugs are entirely necessary and happy provided they are fed plenty of fibre and their environment is not disturbed.

Such disturbances of the body's environment can come in many forms: through the introduction of unwanted bacteria, by taking long-term antibiotics which kill off the good bugs, or by invasive procedures such as colonic irrigation, which should really never be recommended.

A vegetarian diet and drinking vegetable juices and soups is not only highly nutritious but also ideal for the gastrointestinal fauna. Some diets, however, are not always entirely healthy for the body and this is where food safety and hygiene comes in. A recent study into infectious intestinal diseases from a food

THE SEVEN ESSENTIALS OF FOOD HYGIENE

1   Get into the habit of washing your hands before, and particularly after, handling *any* food. This applies particularly to poultry, raw meat, fish and seafood, but also salads, vegetables and eggs.

2   Always wash your hands after handling domestic pets.

3   Kitchen surfaces and cupboards should be regularly cleaned of potentially dangerous bacteria.

4   Wooden chopping boards should be replaced with plastic, if possible; these should then be cleaned after each use.

5   Raw foods should be stored separately from ready-to-eat and cooked foods in the fridge and larder. Always follow the recommended 'use by' date.

6   Fridges should be maintained at a temperature under 5°C (41°F); if necessary, use a fridge thermometer.

7   All taps and telephones should be washed regularly – how often do you stop in the middle of preparing food to answer the telephone?

standards agency showed that as many as 1 in 5 people can expect an episode of diarrhoea and vomiting from food poisoning every year. The chief culprit is known to be campylobacter, which far outweighs the other causes such as salmonella and e.coli. For example, in the UK, all hens carry campylobacter and some 30 per cent carry salmonella as well. Therefore it is really vital – in cleansing and detox programmes especially – that food handling hygiene in the home is absolutely scrupulous.

Those particularly at risk of food poisoning are babies and children under the age of 7, pregnant women (with a risk to the foetus as well), people over the age of 65, and anyone who is ill or who has any immune system deficiency or disorder.

Always wash fresh fruit and vegetables before use; the likelihood is that they have been sprayed with pesticides and walked over by a variety of insects – as well as handled by other people.

Food and drinks to avoid

Our bodies aren't really designed to eat some of the modern foods available today. They can often lead to an accumulation of toxins and fat which can be shifted only through cleansing. Some of these foods contribute to furring of the arteries which makes the body increasingly incapable of circulating freshly oxygenated blood, some cause headaches or jitters, some cause kidney disease, and some simply pile on weight.

Try to cut out or cut down on:
- alcohol
- sweetened drinks
- cakes and biscuits
- coffee
- tea
- red meat (once a week is ample)
- smoke and tar from tobacco
- fried foods
- foods containing white sugar
- white bread
- chocolate
- colas
- convenience foods, cooked or not
- salt (particularly in snacks)
- fast-food take-aways
- sugar and sweets

Although many of us love their taste, none of these foods is actually essential for health. Indeed, our health and energy levels would be greatly improved if we removed them from our diet completely. Take-away foods, the traditional fried breakfast with a mug of tea, old-fashioned puddings and cakes, and fish and chips are all out. So are burgers and chips. If this sounds too depressing, and you simply have to have that chip fix, try switching to oven rather than fried chips. The fact that they are not soaking up large amounts of fat while they cook will certainly help.

Alcohol is a poison, as you will know if you have ever drunk more than your body is already used to. A hangover is actually a sign that the body has been poisoned and is now doing its best to eliminate the toxin. If you have been consuming alcohol, try to remember to drink as much water as you can before you go to bed and then again in the morning when you wake up. This will help to speed up the process of detoxing and make your head and stomach feel a lot better.

Try swopping your usual burger and fries for a more Mediterranean diet, packed with delicious olives and vine tomatoes. Just one or two portions like this per week and you'll be hooked, cleansed – and healthier.

WARNING! SMOKING IS BAD FOR YOUR HEALTH

By far the worst toxins for the human body are tobacco smoke and tobacco tar. The biggest step anyone can take towards optimum health is to give up smoking.

What tobacco smoke contains:

- carcinogens
- carbon monoxide
- nicotine
- radioactive compounds
- hydrogen cyanide
- pesticides
- metals

The effects of smoking on a healthy person include:

- raised blood pressure
- irregular heartbeat
- increased pulse rate
- decreased appetite
- reduced efficiency of red blood cells (which carry oxygen around the body)
- stimulation or depression of nervous system, depending on mood

Over a period of time, smoking also has a bad effect on the arteries, lungs, digestive system and reproductive organs, and in many cases proves fatal.

De-junking the body

There's no magic recipe or pill for cleansing your body. The steps you need to take, however, are straightforward and will significantly improve your health and increase your energy levels.

FIRST STEPS

The skin, the biggest organ of your body, is an excellent indicator of health. It is also the first organ to reveal the need for cleansing. Dietary toxins, such as excess fat, poor nutrition and alcohol in the body all show rapidly on the face.

When you first start cleansing, your skin may erupt as toxins are expelled. Don't worry! This is a good sign; it shows that the waste products and toxins are coming out. Before long your skin will become clearer.

The main steps as you de-junk are watching what you put into your body, eliminating toxins as swiftly as possible by drinking at least eight glasses of water every day and juicing, taking regular brisk exercise and giving the body and brain the opportunity to repair and renew cells during sleep.

JUICING

Most of the body is made up of water, so it can quickly become dehydrated. The vitamins and minerals contained in fruit and uncooked vegetables, together with their high liquid content, make them the ideal food for cleansing and rehydrating the body.

You can pulp or liquidize almost any fruit or vegetable into a delicious drink that is filling as well as being extremely good for your body. You might like to experiment with small quantities of different fruits and vegetables to find the combinations you like the best. Drink the juice from a cup or use a spoon like a purée.

Rapid detoxing may be achieved by eating only one fruit or vegetable for one or two consecutive days – remembering to drink lots of water.

GOOD MIXES FOR JUICING

- cranberry, peach and mango
- papaya and apple
- gooseberry and apple
- radish and cucumber
- spinach and lemon
- pineapple
- melon and nectarine
- lemon and banana
- carrot and beetroot
- cucumber and celery
- banana and kiwi
- rhubarb
- carrot and apple
- carrot and tomato
- cabbage

*Juices can take the place of a
meal or may be drunk before
a meal to clear the system.*

Revitalizing the immune system

The less food is cooked, the better it is for your body and immune system. Equally, the more highly-processed food is, the less likely it is to be nutritious, and the more likely it is to be toxic to you. Boiling your vegetables too much means all their vital nutrients and vitamins are left in the water that you throw away.

In the morning go for wholemeal bread, yoghurt and fruit. Salads, uncooked vegetables, wholemeal pasta and white fish are all excellent for lunch or supper. Most vegetables are much tastier and more potent system cleansers and detoxifiers when eaten uncooked. Good detoxifiers include carrots, baby sweetcorn, broccoli, white cabbage, tomato, mangetout, mushrooms, celery, courgettes, finely chopped onion, shallots and leeks. For optimum cleansing, choose just one vegetable and eat only that for one day.

WARNING SIGNS OF A BODY UNDER STRESS

Do you suffer from recurrent infections such as viruses, flu, spots, thrush or cystitis? Do you put up with regular headaches, migraine or backache? These are warning signs that your body and mind are under stress and that your immune system is failing to meet the challenge of your lifestyle.

Other warning signs of a body under stress include:
- aches and pains
- allergy
- apathy
- asthma
- bloating
- inflammations
- cellulite
- constipation
- dark circles under eyes
- joint swelling and pain
- feeling overtired, sluggish
- feeling tired in the morning
- fluid retention
- blotchy skin/blackheads/whiteheads
- indigestion
- irritable bowel syndrome
- dental abscess
- reduced zest for life
- shortness of breath
- flaring up of eczema

Drink for life – replace lost fluids and cleanse your system throughout the day with water.

WHEN YOU EAT

Stoking up the fire in the morning is a must for a healthy immune system. Making your body run on empty for half the day puts a stress on it, so always find time for breakfast. This really is the most important meal of the day.

HOW OFTEN YOU EAT

It is much easier for the brain and body to function if they are nourished at regular, short intervals. It is better to have six tiny meals a day than two large ones – although this may not always be entirely practicable. Never miss a meal, as this allows toxins to build up in the body, slows down the system and makes reactions duller.

WATER OF LIFE

Fatigue is one of the early warning signs of dehydration, which will, in turn, make the body more vulnerable to catching infections and viruses, and less able to fight them off once they are caught. To feel invigorated, drink a long glass of water first thing in the morning, mid-morning, before lunch, after lunch, mid-afternoon, before supper, after supper and shortly before going to bed.

Exer

Exercise is one of the most important ways in which the body expels toxins and the pollution produced by a chronic build-up of stress and tension.

So taking regular exercise during any cleansing programme is extremely beneficial both mentally and physically. Aerobic exercise is the best as it stimulates the lymphatic system and gets the heart pumping faster. And, as a result:

- more fresh oxygen and nutrients are carried to the body's cells
- the removal of harmful toxins is more efficient
- you become fitter
- you feel better about yourself

cise

Sweating it out

Exercise is an essential element of cleansing because it tones up the systems of the body, including those responsible for the elimination of toxins. We excrete waste matter through the skin by sweating, through the digestive system and through the lymphatic drainage system. The function of the lungs and the circulation is also significantly boosted by regular exercise.

If you exercise moderately for 30 minutes a day, for about three times a week, you will almost halve your risk of a heart attack compared to that of someone who does no exercise at all.

HOW EXERCISE CAN HELP

Exercising to eliminate unwanted and nasty toxins leads to:

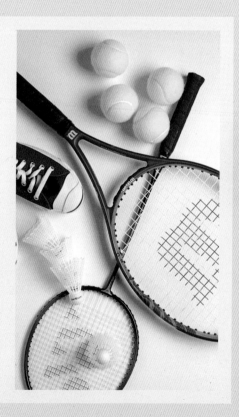

- higher energy levels
- reduced stress and anxiety
- reduced levels of depression
- improved concentration and memory
- increased ability to think through each of your problems
- increased self-confidence and self-esteem
- better quality sleep
- greater resistance to infection
- more flexible joints and muscles
- reduced risk of high blood pressure (by up to 40 per cent)
- reduced risk of heart attack (by over 40 per cent)
- reduced risk of stroke (by 33 per cent)
- reduced risk of diabetes (by 29 per cent)
- possible reduced risk of breast cancer

WHICH TYPE OF EXERCISE IS BEST FOR YOU?

Without a doubt, the best fitness plan for you is what appeals to you the most. What matters is that you enjoy exercise and that you try to do it regularly every week.

You may prefer competitive games, such as tennis, squash, rugby or football. You may prefer more contemplative forms of exercise, such as yoga, t'ai chi, swimming, or hiking in the open countryside. Or you may be attracted to more sociable forms of exercise, such as a workout at the gym or a dance class.

Do you prefer indoor or outdoor exercise? Do you prefer team games or exercising in solitude with time for reflection? Ask yourself these questions, then have a look at the following list and see if one of these activities would be right for you.

aerobics	pilates
Alexander technique	power walking
aquaerobics	rowing
badminton	rugby
boxing	shiatsu
circuit training	skipping
cricket	squash
cycling	step class
fencing	stretch and tone class
football	swimming
golf	t'ai chi
gym	tennis
horse-riding	walking
jogging and running	weight training
movement and dance	yoga

Both your brain and body benefit from regular exercise. It tones up the body and clears the mind. And there is the added benefit that your self-confidence will increase – not only from looking and feeling fitter, but also because you are achieving something important for yourself, which you have done through your own effort.

Remember – no detox programme is complete without the regular exercise which will enable the body to eliminate all those long-stored toxins.

Shape it up

Cleansing helps to dislodge pockets of fat and cellulite. However, for significantly improved body tone and shape, you need to focus on muscular (rather than respiratory and cardiovascular) fitness in your exercise programme.

There are three types of muscle: voluntary muscles, which allow you to move your arms and legs at will; involuntary muscles, which line the blood vessels, stomach, gastrointestinal tract and other internal organs; and the muscles of the heart (the cardiac muscles).

It is the voluntary muscles that you need to work for improved shape and tone. Fortunately, they respond well to exercise, starting to increase in bulk, stamina and strength after only a few weeks' activity. This improvement may correspond with an increase in weight even though overall body measurements will decrease. This is because muscle is denser – and so heavier – than fat.

ACHIEVING MUSCULAR FITNESS

The best route to muscular fitness is an endurance form of exercise rather than one requiring sudden bursts of energy, so go for:

Swimming: Using every muscle group, swimming is excellent for shaping up the body. It can increase shoulder definition, reduce flab on the upper arms and around the waist, tighten up the thighs and calves, and make the ankles trimmer. Regular swimming will substantially improve the functioning of the body's own cleansing system (the lymphatic system, the liver, the kidneys, the lungs and the intestines).

Cycling: Cycling is highly cleansing, as it takes place in the fresh air and is very beneficial to the respiratory system.

Walking: A brisk walk in the fresh air is hard to beat. Walking will improve all types of fitness: muscular, respiratory and cardiovascular. You can do it anywhere, anytime and without any special equipment, so it is easy to incorporate into daily life.

Rowing: This is a great team exercise and is wonderful for toning the cleansing systems of the body and improving your overall shape, especially the upper arms, midriff, abdomen and legs.

Invest in a good bicycle: enjoy the pleasures of getting fit and discovering the countryside around you at the same time.

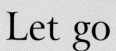
Let go

Relaxing and letting go of troublesome feelings, such as guilt, bitterness, sadness, anxiety and anger, demands exercises for the mind that complement and enhance the cleansing programme for the body. At the same time, such therapies as yoga, t'ai chi and massage also offer undoubted physical benefits.

YOGA

Yoga aims to achieve a state of physical, mental and spiritual well-being through the practice of a series of poses, as well as through conscious relaxation and contemplation.

The poses or postures, known as 'asanas', are practised slowly, with concentration on breathing. This in time creates a sense of inner peace and harmony of body and mind.

A number of different types of yoga are practised in the West, so you will find that classes tend to differ in emphasis and style. Always ask in advance of trying a class about the level of yoga offered and your own suitability for it.

Yoga helps to make the head and neck feel lighter, thus relaxing the mind. Through regular practice the shoulders become less tense, enabling a more efficient blood flow around the body; this, in turn, speeds up the elimination of toxins. Cleansing of lactic acid strengthens the leg muscles, which helps to create a sense of emotional stability.

T'AI CHI

T'ai chi consists of a series of gentle, circular movements (rather like swimming in the air) that exercise the muscles, unify the body and mind, and encourage an even flow of chi (energy) around the body. Inner tensions are released and toxins flow out of the muscles, so that both mind and body benefit from this contemplative and fluid system of exercises.

T'ai chi can improve muscle tone and increase control over the movements of the body. It is also believed to strengthen the gastrointestinal tract, thus aiding the elimination of waste matter.

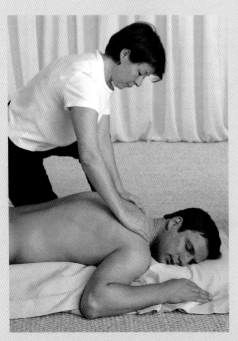

MASSAGE

Massage, acupressure and shiatsu can all be used to achieve physical and mental relaxation. Massage is particularly effective in easing tensions and knotted tissue, increasing the circulation of the blood, and stimulating the lymphatic system, one of the chief routes for ridding the body of toxins.

Take the time to prepare your massage environment properly. Make sure the room is comfortably warm and softly lit – fragranced candles are a good way of lighting the room. Massaging oil and plenty of towels will be needed, and you may like to play some relaxing music.

Work it out

People often think of techniques such as visualization, meditation, self-hypnosis and relaxation as being designed to achieve emotional and spiritual well-being rather than physical.

These techniques have an impact on the physical body as well as the mind, however. As the solutions to problems become clearer, inner tensions are relieved, the body's energy, or chi, starts to flow freely once again, and toxic build-up begins to disperse. As a result, complaints such as headaches, backaches and migraines can diminish as if by magic.

You may feel a little strange to begin with once you start using these techniques, but give it time, and after a while such practices will become an important part of your cleansing routine.

VISUALIZATION
- Lie down in a quiet, darkened room.
- Allow your entire body to relax, limb by limb.
- Stretch and relax your neck and shoulder muscles.
- Start to visualize, bit by bit, the toxins pouring out of your body.
- Imagine a reflexology treatment or foot massage releasing the toxins through your feet and ankles.
- Work upwards through the body so that your leg muscles, digestive system, lymphatic drainage system and skin are cleansed of toxins.

RELAXATION
- Lie on your back in a quiet room and allow each muscle of your body to relax.
- Stretch out your ankles and relax them. Flex your shoulder muscles and let them go.
- Lengthen, then release your torso.
- Wiggle your fingers.
- Now empty your mind and just lie still for about 30 minutes. If you find it hard to empty your mind, focus your thoughts on your breathing.

Relaxation is a semi-conscious state, not sleep, so be sure to stay awake!

SELF-HYPNOSIS

A couple of sessions with a hypnotherapist is the best way to learn self-hypnosis. Decide what you would like to focus on with your hypnotherapist and allow her or him to take you into a deep trance-like state. Successful hypnosis achieves a completely purified, cleansed state in which you are free of anxiety and tension.

MEDITATION

Imagine yourself on a beach on a clear, sunny day with a little breeze blowing. The sea air courses through your nose and mouth, down your oesophagus and into your respiratory system. Feel your lungs expelling the toxins of traffic-laden air and inhaling the fresh sea breezes. Concentrate now on the fresh air and nothing else. Hold this focus for about 20 minutes, while keeping your body entirely relaxed. Allow yourself to feel the breath flowing in and out of your body.

Visualize yourself lying on a deserted beach and breathing the clean sea air deep into your body, washing out all tension, stress and toxins with the outward breath.

Sleeping on it

After all that exercise, your body needs a total rest. The body is reinvigorated by sleep. During the day, little by little, we are – literally – worn out. It is at night that the billions of cells in the body are most rapidly renewed. (Although this renewal also takes place during waking hours, the process is much slower.)

The brain and nervous system are rested and refreshed during sleep because we are unable to react to what is going on around us. Most bodily processes slow down: we use less oxygen, our temperature falls and our heart rate slows.

As we sleep, the body's natural cleansing systems – the liver, the kidneys and the circulation – carry on with their work unimpeded by further onslaughts of harmful toxins.

Without enough sleep, we feel tired, sluggish and bleary. Our metabolism becomes slow so that when we eat – perhaps in an attempt to acquire more energy – we burn fewer calories than we would if we were well rested. Because we are not ready to wake up, our eyes feel dry (the production of tear liquid decreases during sleep); our skin is dry and itchy, our legs ache, and we may feel cold, shivery, apathetic and unable to concentrate.

Sleep is an essential element of any exercise programme and a fundamental part of detoxing and cleansing. Without good-quality, regular sleep the body will not benefit as much from the steps that you take to cleanse it.

The mind, in particular, needs sleep in order to switch off and recharge. Problems are discharged and often resolved during sleep and what may have seemed a muddle or a problem during the day becomes clear the following day after a good night's sleep. The brain slows down during contemplation and meditative relaxation . . . but nothing beats sleep.

WHAT IS GOOD SLEEP?

Good quality sleep depends on:
- going to bed at roughly the same time each night and getting up at roughly the same time each morning
- avoiding food or stimulants such as tea, coffee, alcohol or nicotine for three hours before bedtime
- sleeping in a well-ventilated room, preferably with a window slightly open

Work out your sleep pattern and try to stick to it. Your body will benefit from a routine, leaving you feeling refreshed when you wake in the morning.

- sleeping in a room free of distractions such as a computer, TV, newspapers or work papers
- sleeping on a bed that gives you good support but is not too hard
- sleeping in a quiet environment (using earplugs if need be)
- putting off stimulating discussions with your partner or family until the following day
- resisting the temptation to get up and make a cup of tea if you cannot sleep

IF YOU CANNOT SLEEP

If sleep will not come, lie calmly and visualize the cells of the body renewing themselves. When you rest in a dark room, the body, though not the brain, is capable of some regeneration. For the brain to benefit, sleep is essential.

Beautiful

Indulge yourself by pampering your body in myriad different ways for a fully cleansed, refreshed finish.

Take a good look at the state of your skin, hair and nails. If you don't like what you see, perhaps it's time to think about looking after yourself a bit more. You may like to:

- exfoliate the skin
- treat yourself – cleanse from top to toe
- experiment with aromatic oils

Body

Smoothing the rough bits

The skin plays an important role in cleansing the body by eliminating unwanted toxins through sweating. Any blockage in this process, in the form of blocked pores, spots, blackheads, whiteheads and dead or old hard skin, impairs the body's natural cleansing system.

BLEMISHES

Blocked pores, spots, blackheads and whiteheads are most likely to be seen on the face. The best ways to avoid these blemishes are scrupulous cleansing every morning and every night, drinking plenty of cold water and taking regular exercise in the fresh air. Never pick or pop spots – no matter how tempting it might be – and never hack off old skin with scissors or a nail file.

DEAD SKIN

Dead skin is often found on the elbows, and can be removed with exfoliation creams, available from a pharmacy. Hard skin on the feet is best treated by chiropody or pedicure.

Dead skin is sloughed off continually; the body's cleansing system therefore benefits greatly from dry skin brushing (brushing with an exfoliating mitt) before you take a bath or shower. Start by brushing the back of the neck, move on to the shoulders, arms, hands, back, front, bottom, and finally brush your legs

and your feet. Use a special facial mitt for your face, as body mitts may be too coarse for its more delicate skin, and damage it.

DRY BRUSHING

Dry brushing can help to bring a fresh bloom to the skin as old dead cells are brushed off. The pores can breathe properly once again, and waste matter can escape efficiently through perspiration.

DRY SKIN

Dry skin brushing not only invigorates the skin but it also helps to revive the circulation, which brings freshly oxygenated blood to all parts of the body, increasing your vitality and bloom. If you suffer from cold hands and feet in the winter, dry skin brushing is an effective means of restoring your blood circulation to the extremities.

Try making your own exfoliation creams using natural and enriching ingredients such as ground-up nuts and cereals, or salt with honey.

Making your own beauty products means you can create natural creams and tonics that suit your body's cleansing needs exactly.

Top-to-toe cleansing

Before you start your top-to-toe cleansing programme, go for a 20-minute run or a brisk walk which will help to bounce all the body's natural cleansing systems into action.

HAIR

Everybody's hair washing needs and wants are different – some people prefer to wash their hair every day, while others find their hair is not suited to frequent washing. Hair care experts recommend that you try to vary your hair products every few months for optimum cleansing and conditioning. Avoid using combined shampoos and conditioners, as they may leave unwanted deposits in your hair, leaving it feeling dank and dull, and on your scalp, causing irritation.

EARS

Avoid inserting anything into your ears. Wash them with a wet flannel. If you feel that your hearing is not too good or you suffer occasional dizzy spells, see your family doctor – your ears may need syringing.

REFLEXOLOGY

One of the most stimulating complementary therapies is reflexology. It sharpens up the body's immune system, raises energy levels by releasing energy blockages and, above all, hastens the elimination of waste products.

ORAL CLEANSING

Teeth should be cleaned twice daily by first using dental floss and a good quality toothbrush.

If you use an electric toothbrush and gums bleed, go gently but don't stop using it. Note, however, that bleeding gums are usually a sign that bacteria are lurking and the gums have become spongy.

HYDROTHERAPY

This includes any technique or therapy that uses water. It is, of course, ideal for top-to-toe cleansing.

Hydrotherapy methods include steam (Turkish) bath, sauna, jacuzzi (whirlpool bath), salt bath, mineral bath (available from a pharmacy), cider vinegar bath or bath with aromatherapy oils.

MASSAGE

Self-massage, massage by your partner or a friend, and professional massage are excellent mind and body cleansers. Massage helps to stimulate the lymphatic drainage system and boosts the circulation. (See page 25 for further information.)

STEAMING

Steam inhalation is an excellent facial cleanser. Add a couple of drops of essential oil to a bowl of boiling water, cover your head with a towel and inhale the steam for 5 minutes.

HANDY CLEANSING TRAVEL PACK

When you travel always take with you:

- packet of moist towelettes for cleaning and rehydrating the face and hands
- foot spray for refreshing the feet
- toothbrush and toothpaste
- bottle of water to prevent dehydration and fatigue

Aromatherapy

This is a deliciously luxurious way of cleansing. The aromatherapy oils selected here have all been chosen for their cleansing, invigorating and uplifting properties.

Using essential oils is rapidly becoming one of the most popular forms of natural therapy ever, with many of us using an oil every day for its healing or cleansing properties.

Oils enter the bloodstream through the skin and/or the nose and are best known for their use in aromatherapy massage, but they also penetrate through the skin's surface when used in the bath or in skincare products.

And thanks to the variety of oils widely available to the ordinary consumer, their applications are never-ending – whether used for lifting and clearing a bad mood in order to cleanse your mind, or as a soothing cream for the body.

Essential oils are absorbed through the skin at molecular level, passing through the hair follicles and diffusing into the bloodstream and cellular fluids. Depending on how much body fat you have, these oils can take anything from 20 minutes to several hours to be absorbed.

METHODS

1 Add a couple of drops of your favourite essential oil to your bath.
2 Use a vaporizer or diffuser containing a sensuous oil.
3 Add a few drops of calming geranium essential oil to a bowl of boiling water and inhale it.
4 Choose an essential oil and use it in a burner.
5 Massage the whole body with a couple of drops of oil added to a carrier oil, such as olive, sunflower, sweet almond, peach or apricot kernel oil.
6 Use an essential oil in a compress on the forehead if you have a headache or are feeling stressed.
7 Add a refreshing and moisturizing oil to a foot bath.

SMUDGE STICKS

A variation on using oils for aromatherapy, smudge sticks are made from dried herbs, such as sage, tied together in small bundles. Light your stick and place on a heat-resistant surface, such as a dinner plate, then simply soak up the invigorating and cleansing aroma.

Versatile and inspiring – use essential oils or smudge sticks to relax, invigorate and unclog your mind.

CLEANSING FOR BODY & SPIRIT

Oils to choose from

There are many essential oils to choose from, and you may decide to consult an aromatherapist who can suggest a number of oils for you as an individual, taking into account any aches, pains and disorders or allergies that you may have.

The following oils have been chosen for their general suitability in a cleansing programme and are listed together with some of their specific additional properties.

OIL	USES
bergamot	relaxing and energizing; relieves nausea, flatulence, menstrual pain
chamomile	relaxing, antiseptic, anti-inflammatory; relieves menstrual pain, flatulence, general stress and irritability, eczema and allergies
cypress	relaxing; relieves aching joints and heavy periods
eucalyptus	antiseptic, deodorizing, stimulating; calms irritation; excellent for catarrh and bronchitis taken in steam inhalation
fennel	weak diuretic, relaxing; relieves flatulence and constipation
geranium	calming, astringent; useful in treating diarrhoea, haemorrhoids, ulcers, dysentery and dry skin
jasmine	relaxing; useful aphrodisiac and for dry skin conditions
juniper	antiseptic, diuretic, stimulating, relaxing; sometimes useful for treating cystitis, also good for acne
lavender	soothing, sedating, antiseptic; relieves flatulence, repels insects
lemon	tonic, soothing, cleansing, antioxidizing, astringent; particularly useful for colds and flu
neroli	calming, antioxidizing
orange	antispasmodic, sedating; useful for constipation and tension headaches
peppermint	stimulating, antiseptic, antispasmodic, anti-inflammatory; especially useful in relieving menstrual pain
pine	counter-irritant; especially useful in steam inhalation for coughs, laryngitis, bronchitis, catarrh and asthma
rose	tonic, laxative, diuretic, astringent; good as an anti-depressant
rosemary	tonic, calming, diuretic, antispasmodic, antiseptic
tea tree	effective for fungal infections such as thrush, and for skin problems

*Lemon is helpful when your body is feeling run down,
as a treatment for greasy skin or as a cold and flu remedy.*

DON'TS

- Never use oils undiluted. Use a suitable base or carrier oil, such as almond oil, and dilute as per your aromatherapist's instructions, or as on the oil bottle.
- Don't use homoeopathic remedies at the same time as aromatherapy oils.
- Don't use any oils that have toxic properties: armoise, arnica, baldo leaf, bitter almond, calamus, horseradish, jaborandi, leaf mustard, pennyroyal, rue, sassafras, savin, southernwood, tansy, thuja, wintergreen, wormwood.
- If you are pregnant or intending to be so, don't use any of the above oils, or angelica, aniseed and oregano. Be sure to consult a trained aromatherapist.
- Never buy cheap oils. Look for products that are described as 'pure essential oil' and not simply labelled 'aromatherapy oil'.

Natural facelift

Health and happiness are the foundation stones of an attractive appearance, but there are also steps that you can take to help things along. Fresh, healthy, natural foods, lots of exercise and good sleep all help good health to glow and radiate from you.

There are a few golden rules that you should try to follow:

- protect against wrinkles by using a moisturizer
- never pick at blackheads, whiteheads, spots, pimples or insect bites
- de-stress with essential aromatic oils first thing in the morning
- exfoliate regularly in order to remove dead cells and speed up the elimination of toxins
- don't put on any make-up for the first couple of hours in the morning, when you will still be looking pale; wait until you have regained your colour and you will not need to apply so much
- get active with the tweezers first thing in the morning, when you are less likely to feel pain
- in sunny weather, try to avoid going out after 11.30 a.m. without sunscreen to protect the face
- fruit and vegetables are essential for a healthy looking skin; eat plenty for breakfast and some with lunch and dinner; when you feel like a snack, perhaps in the mid-afternoon, go for apple and celery or radish and cucumber, for example
- take care of that afternoon shine with a splash of cold water and a gentle toner; then use a moisturizer containing antioxidants
- exercise every day in order to tone up the circulation and eliminate toxins
- avoid using perfume, bleach (for facial hair) or detergent on the facial skin.
- fresh air every day is a must for healthy-looking skin
- aromatherapy facial massage (using upward strokes) is a delicious treat – ideally practise every day
- visualization, meditation and the Alexander Technique are all effective methods of relaxation – and relaxation is vital to prevent wrinkles forming
- cleansing and moisturizing before going to bed are essential in order to remove the pollution of the day and the toxins excreted by your facial skin

Try to avoid stress as much as possible, or
it will show on your face

- beauty sleep is not a myth; when you sleep, your body repairs itself; the epidermis is in a continuous phase of regrowth, and cell division more than doubles at night, so sleep is vital for bodily regeneration
- stimulants such as caffeine and alcohol, and toxins such as tobacco smoke and tobacco tar, are ruinous to the complexion – kick the habit; all cause unsightly thread veins on the face and, over many years, lead to leathery, wrinkled skin
- always wear comfortable shoes; painful feet show in the face, causing frowns and wrinkles
- a deep-cleansing facial is a must every now and again; treat yourself to a professional one the first time and then do it yourself – pure luxury!
- finally – and most importantly – smile!

Cleansing
THE

Sorting out problems, resolving dilemmas, getting to the bottom of what causes you stress and de-junking your life all help you to think clearly and have renewed energy.

The mind can be a powerful thing – sometimes leading you to believe that your goals are unreachable and your problems are insurmountable. However, with a little cleansing and re-evaluating of priorities, you really can feel more in control. Take a look at the following:

- energy boosters
- dealing with stress
- taking a new view of your worries
- thinking positively

Mind

Energy boosters

It is so common for us to feel tired all the time that family doctors abbreviate the condition as TATT in patients' medical notes. But it doesn't have to be like that; you can regain your energy and start living life to the full once again. First of all, assess your life.

Look at the three principal areas of your life:
- your work life (paid and unpaid)
- your social and family life
- your personal life, when you have time to yourself

A GOOD BALANCE?

Are you able to spend time with close friends and family? Do you get time to do those things that refresh you and recharge your batteries – things that do not fall into the task or relationship categories?

Balance in life is essential if you are to reach your potential and enjoy life without feeling constantly drained. Be generous to yourself: give yourself time to read, get out in the fresh air, go to a film or do whatever you enjoy. Once you have made time for yourself, you will have the energy to meet the challenges of the other areas of your life.

RAPID ENERGY BOOSTERS

- regular dance class – perhaps at your local adult education institute
- laugh with a comic novel or film
- long walk by the seashore or through the countryside
- vigorous game of tennis or squash
- helping hand for someone you know is in need – they may require company, or help with a home or garden task; just offer – what you give out is what you get back
- painting or drawing
- planning a wonderful surprise for a close friend or your partner
- session in a flotation tank
- consultation with an osteopath or chiropractor

DON'TS

- avoid spreading yourself too thin, or you and everyone around you will suffer
- avoid trying to buck yourself up with coffee, chocolate or crisps. In the long run they will make you feel more tired
- don't feel that you have to take on everything you are asked to do. Learn how to say no, for the sake of your physical and emotional health

Do you need to:
- sort out long-term problems?
- banish negative forces from your life?
- resolve dilemmas?
- de-junk your life or home of clutter?
- take the window boxes/plants/ garden in hand?
- organize your workloads?
- spend more time with your loved ones?

To accomplish this:
- reassess your belief in yourself and try to raise your self-esteem
- deal with on-going stresses in your life, rather than ignoring them
- examine your core beliefs and try to make positive changes to your lifestyle
- take a 'clean broom' to your life with renewed positive energy and outlook

Gardening is all about nurturing life, and as your plants are cared for, you'll find your mind will be too.

45

Your thinking style

Many of us lack the faith in ourselves to do what we want to do. We tend to underestimate our own intelligence and ability to achieve our goals in life. Don't sell yourself short.

Women in particular tend to set their sights too low for their abilities. This can often be seen in their choice of job and partner. Women typically attribute their successes to luck, good fortune, being in the right place at the right time or sheer hard work – but not to their own talent.

People often hold back from doing what they can see needs to be done because of fear of rejection and failure. Fear is poisonous to the spirit; listen to your gut reactions. Do what you want to do because it feels right for you.

Assertiveness is essential to success in all areas of your life but it is often mistaken for aggression, particularly in women. Society does not punish women for statements of incompetence and failure, whereas it sees those same statements as wimpish if made by a man. It is vital to stand up for yourself and to be prepared to risk failure in order to achieve self-fulfilment. Many women need to understand that being tougher does not conflict with being caring and feminine.

Low self-esteem can be crippling and can mean that you do not have the confidence to make decisions. If you lack self-esteem you may find yourself trapped in a situation where you are very unhappy, such as a loveless partnership or an unsatisfying job, but in which you are still unable to make changes for the better. There is no guarantee that if you take steps towards big changes and a better life it will all turn out to be lovely. It may not. But at least you will have tried – and you may be agreeably surprised.

If you sell yourself short, others will undervalue you, too. If you don't feel you're worth anything, how can you expect anyone else to? Never run yourself down: if you keep saying

WORK ON YOURSELF

If there are things that you don't like about yourself, work on them by curbing those traits and developing other more positive ones. If you have an obvious fault, such as always being late, resolve to do something about it and see how much better you feel about yourself.

We cannot change our fundamental personality, of course, but we can modify bad habits.

things like: 'Oh, well, I'm no good at that' – then people will start to believe you.

How many times do you hear women, especially, saying: 'I don't really understand cars', or 'I'm a technophobe', for example? Have faith in yourself and others will, too.

<u>**KEY POINTS:**</u>
- only apologise if you're in the wrong
- believe in yourself
- do all jobs to the best of your ability
- always remember that other people may be unsure of themselves too
- sleep on things if you're not sure of the right course of action

I can deal calmly with difficult situations.

My partner and I are handling our problems.

I live a rich and fulfilling life.

I am being paid well to do a rewarding job.

I am in control of my life.

I mix well with other people.

AFFIRMATIONS

Affirmations are short statements about yourself or your life you want to change. Write them down, putting them where they may be seen easily: on the fridge, notice board or a computer screen saver. By writing them down, you imprint a positive message on your subconscious. Keep them in the present tense and always use positive language.

Overcoming stress

Stress is toxic to both body and mind. When we are stressed, certain brain chemicals are activated, setting off a very complex set of physical, as well as mental, chain reactions.

DISORDERS CAUSED BY STRESS-RELATED REACTIONS:

- headache
- eczema
- depression
- raised blood pressure
- chronic fatigue

- migraine
- unexplained anger
- anxiety
- apathy
- stroke

- backache
- asthma
- sneezing fits
- heart attack

There are many different causes of stress – the necessity of staying in a job you dislike, an unsatisfactory family relationship, divorce, bereavement, lack of money, ill health or simply too much to do in too little time. The key to alleviating stress is three-fold: prioritize, eliminate, delegate.

PRIORITIZE

Sit and write down everything you have to do in order of importance to *you*. Of these priorities, are there some that you can eliminate or put on the back burner? Which of your priorities can you delegate to others? You don't have to do everything yourself. By having a careful look at your priorities in this way you can reduce your workload and start to overcome stress. Take control!

ELIMINATE

Not everything we do in our work, family and personal life necessarily has to be done. Scrutinize your list to see what can be eliminated, thus freeing up some of your time.

DELEGATE

Friends, family and paid help can all assist in reducing your workload. Never be afraid to ask for help, especially at times of stress – this is not a sign of weakness. In fact, it can sometimes take great courage to ask for help from someone else – so don't feel as though you are failing. Other people really like to be asked and to feel needed. If they feel as if they are helping you to cope better and become calmer, they will feel a great sense of achievement as well.

Once you have unlocked the causes of stress in your life, you can start to take control by resolving dilemmas, cutting out dead wood and setting goals.

One of the greatest causes of stress is unresolved dilemmas, which may drag on for years. For example, money worries, an unsatisfactory marriage or relationship, a friendship that causes irritation rather than joy, a hobby that was once a pleasure but has turned into a chore or a job you dislike.

Are there aspects of your life which invariably stress you? What steps can you take to eliminate or resolve them? Now is the time to set boundaries, to tell yourself that you do not have to

Piles of papers and unwanted clutter stress all of us – make time for your dreaded filing and create some extra storage space.

put up with this situation or behaviour. You deserve better. By knowing that you deserve better, you will be able to achieve improvements in all areas of your life.

You cannot, of course, achieve everything at once; in some situations you may have to set intermediate goals and monitor your progress.

By taking control of your life like this, you are already part of the way to overcoming stress and cleansing your mind and body of harmful toxins.

Cognitive therapy

Talking to a friend when you are stressed can be of tremendous value. Some forms of psychotherapy are very like this, although the therapist – unlike the friend – is not expected to find solutions or make judgements.

The aim of cognitive therapy and some other psychotherapies is for the therapist to help the client modify their feelings, views and ideas about themselves. Another feature, common to all psychotherapies, is that the therapist is not there to find answers to your problems. He or she allows you to find your own solutions through the technique of exploratory discussion. Developing your own strategies helps you to mature and develop your inner strength, thus building the foundations for managing your life in the future.

Psychotherapy is no easy option. It requires motivation, commitment, time and, in many countries, money. Cognition describes thinking, memory and perception. Cognitive therapy can be defined as help with how we view events and situations in life. Because how we think determines how we feel, the premise is that by modifying our automatic reactions and thoughts (or 'hot thoughts'), we can alter our feelings and moods.

If you feel that you could benefit from this type of professional help, your family doctor will be able to refer you to a psychologist or psychiatrist who specializes in cognitive therapy. Everything that you discuss remains totally confidential, just as with a doctor. It is important for all of us to be able to talk to someone about problems, issues and feelings from time to time, and sometimes we need that little bit of extra help that only a trained professional can offer.

COGNITIVE THERAPY IS ESPECIALLY SUITABLE FOR:

- problems of low self-esteem
- patterns of destructive behaviour, e.g. alcoholism, uncontrollable anger or depression
- people who have recurrent emotional problems and relationship difficulties
- people who have developed a negative and defeatist attitude towards themselves so that any adversity in their life can provoke a major crisis

Depression

It is important to acknowledge that, sometimes, you may feel more than just a little stressed. If you are starting to feel as though you really can't cope with even the most simple of everyday tasks, you could be suffering from early signs of depression.

You may cry at the thought of getting out of bed or feel panicky when choosing which colour shirt to wear. Obviously, these straightforward events should not be making you feel this way – but they could be a physical indication that something more serious is going on inside your mind.

Depression can be difficult to treat and any regime undertaken should be as holistic as possible in its approach and tailored to your specific circumstances.

HERBAL REMEDIES

As well as consulting a therapist, you might also like to consider trying a natural therapy. Used worldwide for a variety of ailments, herbal remedies are fast becoming one of the most popular natural alternatives in place of conventional medicine.

You can obtain herbal remedies from most chemists and good health stores. They should, however, only be used under the supervision of a qualified herbalist.

The following herbs are particularly suitable for the treatment of depression:

- *St John's Wort:* general anti-depressive effects and used as a sedative
- *Ginkgo biloba:* stimulates the blood supply to the brain, improves cognition
- *Kava-kava:* for mild anxiety and depression; also mildly sedating
- *Borage:* nervous depression and grief
- *Basil:* general antidepressant – oil often used during massage for depression

Borage, renowned as a herbal pick-me-up, is available as a juice or tincture for treating depression.

Positive environment

With the new-found energy you have gained from assessing your lifestyle and examining your core beliefs, now is the time to bring a bright new positive focus to bear on your surroundings both at home and at work – for your mind, body and spirit.

Our surroundings are of inestimable power and value to us as individuals. A happy warm atmosphere spells out the message that someone cares in this home about the people that live there and the fabric of the home. Look very critically at your environment, as if it were actually someone else's, and consider whether or not you like it. If you do, fine, if you don't, now is the time to start making changes. And, you don't have to do it all at once. If there is lots to do, draw up a programme, so that you achieve one target by the autumn, one during winter, and another by spring and so on. Set yourself achievable goals and targets.

AT HOME

Start going through your home, room by room, sorting out clutter – unwanted presents, out-of-date telephone directories, broken tapes and scratched records, empty jam jars, ancient newspapers, millions of supermarket carrier-bags, food past its sell-by date, old coat-hangers, out-of-date reference books, underwear that long ago gave up the ghost, old shoes and wellington boots, cardboard boxes, radios that don't work, empty or broken ball-point pens, dead house plants, broken flowerpots and all the rest of the junk.

Ask yourself as you go from cupboard to cupboard, room by room: is it decorative? Is it functional? If it's neither, bin it.

YOUR WARDROBE

It is said that we wear 20 per cent of our clothes 80 per cent of the time, so . . . get out all your clothes and sort them into four big piles:

1 definitely want to keep
2 so old it can only be worn for gardening or go in the bin
3 not sure – needs a second look
4 needs attention – dry-cleaning, washing, mending or altering

From pile **3** pick out one or two 'must keeps' and give the rest to charity. Now take another look at pile **1** and see if you can make it smaller by asking yourself these questions:

Does it still fit? If not, alter it, throw it away or give it to charity. Would I give good money for it if I saw it for sale in a shop now, or have I worn it in the last three years? If not, throw it away or give it to charity.

YOUR WORK
(at home or out of the home, paid or unpaid)
- make your environment pleasant with plants and pictures
- clean the windows
- check or service your tools
- update your contacts/address book
- sort out all papers – either throw them away, deal with them or file them

Cleansing is partly a state of mind; give yourself the right environment and you are halfway there. Get rid of what you don't want and enjoy what you have. And remember – *you can do anything you decide to do*.

FENG SHUI

Feng Shui – meaning 'wind and water' is the ancient oriental art of object placement aimed to increase the positive effects on your health, career, wealth, love life and spirit self. This practice is based on the movement of *chi* – the 'energy of life' that is said to exist all around us.

As its benefits are recognized worldwide, many people rely on Feng Shui as second nature to organize their home environment. In addition, more and more businesses are turning to Feng Shui experts to create the most positive and therefore more work-efficient offices.

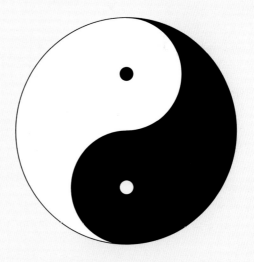

The oriental symbol of Yin-Yang, denoting balance of the universe.

Cleansing

AND

*L*et cleansing become a regular part of your life by assigning one day every week to ridding your body and mind of accumulated toxins.

Start with a detox weekend, or, if you have been ill or stressed, an entire week. This is true luxury for both body and spirit – and you deserve it. Why not try:

- a one-day detox – a great first sample on detoxing
- a weekend detox programme
- a full detox holiday

Detox
Programmes

Detox for a day

This is a great way to try detoxing yourself if you haven't tried to before. Try doing this on a weekend day, perhaps even ask some friends to join you, and – above all – enjoy it!

WHEN YOU WAKE UP

- glass of water with a slice of lemon
- 1 slice of wholemeal bread without butter to really wake up the digestive system
- 30 minutes' brisk exercise such as walking or running to speed up your circulatory system, which assists in lymph drainage
- a smoothie – a glass of liquidized fruit or vegetables
- dry skin brushing before bath or shower to remove dead cells, and exfoliation cream for face, hands, feet and elbows
- steam inhalation to speed up facial cleansing as toxins are expelled through your pores
- two glasses of water to help flush out unwanted toxins
- bath or shower with aromatic essential oils
- wash hair and treat your body to a massage afterwards
- game of tennis – or whatever exercise appeals to you
- another glass of water
- salt rub after exercise to help slough off dead skin and speed up the detox process

(If you prefer, forget sports today and turn out all the kitchen cupboards.)

LATE MORNING

- glass of water

LUNCH TIME

- glass of water
- anything you like from the following: salad, fruit, vegetables, pulses (beans and lentils), wholemeal bread

MID-AFTERNOON

- two glasses of water with a slice of lemon
- one hour in some form of relaxation or relaxing exercise such as meditation, yoga, self-hypnosis or t'ai chi
- stick of celery or an apple if you prefer
- one hour assessing your lifestyle and making a list of changes you wish to achieve
- make a cleansing soup such as carrot and tomato, white bean and lemon, broccoli or whatever vegetables and pulses appeal, and eat with wholemeal bread

EARLY EVENING

- glass of water
- 20 minutes skipping
- 20 minutes stretch and tone exercises

MID-EVENING

- glass of water
- thoroughly cleanse and moisturize your face and apply exfoliating cream once again to your hands
- check that your bedroom conforms with the tips for good quality sleep (see pages 28–29)
- go to bed at least an hour earlier than usual, certainly by 11.00 p.m.

BEFORE BED

- glass of water

Salads are excellent to include in any detox programme. Keep them simple and avoid a dressing if you possibly can.

Detox for the weekend

You can eat what you like for the whole weekend so long as it comprises salads, vegetables, pulses or fruits. You may prefer to eat every two or three hours, taking perhaps as many as five small meals rather than two or three big ones. It is best not to eat for three hours before bedtime but be sure to drink plenty of water.

WATER

You will need to drink 11 to 12 glasses of water a day, as you did for the one-day detoxing programme. Many of us are happy to drink water from the tap. For those living in cities where the water may not taste that good, bottled water may be preferable.

You will need to take a bottle of water with you when you exercise, particularly if you are out walking on a warm day.

If you were to go to a health spa for the weekend, your programme would look something like this:

Exercise is important in any detox regime.

WHEN YOU WAKE UP

- a glass of water and lemon
- 3–6.5-km (2–4-mile) walk before breakfast, or 20–30-minute swim
- breakfast: wholemeal bread, yoghurt, fruit juice, muesli, fresh fruit, dried fruit, decaffeinated coffee or tea, both without milk
- aromatherapy facial massage
- one hour exercise class
- steam room and sauna for a total of 40 minutes
- relax in a hot dark room wrapped in warm towels for 10–15 minutes
- salt rub
- walk or table tennis for up to an hour before lunch

LUNCH
- own selection from fruit juices, different salads (including vegetables, pastas and pulses), wholemeal bread, hard cheeses, grilled fish, chicken, fruits, decaffeinated coffee or tea (no milk or sugar)
- relax with a book or music for up to an hour
- exercise class
- yoga or other form of detoxing and relaxation

TEA
- decaffeinated, with a slice of lemon
- gym for one hour

SUPPER
- from the same sort of foods as lunch; hot dishes could include soup, pasta in various sauces, grilled fish; and desserts such as rhubarb crumble made with brown sugar and wholemeal flour.
- cards, reading, concert or TV
- short relaxing swim or jacuzzi before bedtime

The second day might incorporate a longer walk in the morning, and you might decide to swap the exercise classes for squash or an hour in the gym. Exercise classes may be stretch and tone, step, aerobics or power yoga.

Yoga is an effective way of relaxing and detoxing both mind and body.

You can see that there is a good mix of activities with time allowed for rest and recuperation, when you will have the opportunity of cleansing your mind. This is what you should aim for in a detox weekend. Ideally, cut out the fish, chicken and cheeses, as this detox is just for two days. Virtually everything that a health spa has to offer, you can do yourself at home and at your local leisure centre.

KEY POINTS

Try to keep the following in mind for the most beneficial detox:

- include good mix of activities to keep your mind focused
- avoid outside distractions or commitments
- drink plenty of water
- get an early night

Detox holiday: one week

Some people view detox as nothing more than a fast, but detox is in fact healthier and safer than fasting which completely disrupts the digestive system and your metabolism. If you find yourself attracted to the idea of fasting, do it just for one day, perhaps on successive Saturdays, or on a day of the week when you are not working, driving or operating heavy machinery.

A detox week seems like real luxury for most of us and yet it is within the reach of us all if we elect to take a week's holiday. A detox week, or a week at a health spa, is much more revitalizing than any other sort of holiday, including a week on a warm beach or a week skiing.

All you need is free time and a good programme of activities so that you don't become bored.

Before you embark on your week, think of all the things that you would really like to do and see if you can incorporate some of them into your detox week. For example, going to the sea or the country, to an art gallery, a concert, or a craft fair, or whatever appeals to you – so long as you remember to take a bottle of water with you.

You could earmark one day for detoxing your home environment (see pages 52–53), a second day for dealing with all the letters and bills that may have piled up and a third day to complete a 10-mile (16-km) walk – provided that you have already completed several 5–6-mile (8–10-km) walks. You could allocate a fourth day to getting started on a big project which might otherwise be put off, for example, planning your garden, redecorating a room, repotting your house plants or sticking ten years' worth of photos into albums.

You don't have to be inactive just because you are detoxing; in fact, activity will increase and enhance the cleansing process. Take as much exercise as you can. Walking for up to three hours a day is fine if you don't fancy anything too strenuous.

Remember to drink about a dozen glasses of water a day and not to let a drop of caffeinated coffee or tea, or alcohol touch your lips. If you have suddenly come off alcohol and caffeine, you may suffer from disturbed sleep at night and, perhaps, headaches during the day. Don't worry, nothing is wrong; these are symptoms from all the toxins that you normally flood your body with and they will pass within days.

You may decide on the first day of your detox week to drink only the juice of vegetables and fruits rather than take any solid food. This will give the cleansing and detox process a head start. You could also do this on the third or fourth day of your detox week, but don't do it on successive days unless you are very fit, healthy and young.

The day before you start your detox week, visit your local greengrocer, an organic farm shop and the largest local supermarket to check out the choice of vegetables and fruit. Buy enough for just two or three days and no more, as these foods deteriorate very quickly.

Try going away for a holiday away in the mountains for your detox week. The clean air at the higher altitude and the scenery will offer both your body and your mind an instant cleanse.

You don't have to be a non-meat eater to sample vegetarian food. Vegetarian meals are delicious as well as being the best way to round off the perfect detox week.

Take a look through several vegetarian cookbooks for ideas for making soups, interesting salads and vegetable casseroles. Get in a good choice of essential oils to burn in a vaporizer or burner.

Key points for your detox week:
- lots of exercise
- get rid of all the clutter at home
- salt bath once during the week
- lots of fresh air
- lots and lots of water
- some relaxation
- exfoliation
- lots of swimming
- several small meals

NB – don't embark on a detox week if you feel unwell or are menstruating, pregnant or breastfeeding.

One week of detox and you will probably find yourself amazed at the improvement in the condition of your skin and hair and your feelings of improved self-esteem and confidence – all of which add up to greatly increased energy, productivity and creativity.

Useful contacts

The following organizations will be able to supply information and equipment on all aspects of cleansing and detox:

In the UK
Action on Smoking and Health (ASH)
109 Gloucester Place
London W1H 3PH
Tel: 44 (0)20 7935 3519

Alcoholics Anonymous (AA)
PO Box 1, Stonebow House
Stonebow
York YO1 2NJ
Tel: 44 (0)1904 644026

Aromatherapy Organizations Council
PO Box 355
Croydon CR9 2QP
Tel: 44 (0)20 8251 7912

British Wheel of Yoga
1 Hamilton Place, Boston Road
Sleaford, Lincolnshire NG34 7ES
Tel: 44 (0)1529 306851

*The General Council and Register
of Naturopaths*
2 Goswell Road, Street
Somerset BA16 0JG
Tel: 44 (0)1458 840072

Institute for Complementary Medicine
PO Box 194
London SE16 1QZ
Tel: 44 (0)20 7237 5165

In the US
*Iyengar Yoga National Association
of the United States*
Tel: 1 800 889 9642
www.comnet.org/iynaus

National Centre for Homoeopathy
801 N Fairfax Street
Alexandria
VA 22314
Tel: 1 703 548 7790

In Australia
*Complementary Medical Association
Inc.,*
Suite 20, 1 Gladstone Road, Castle
Hill 2154 NSW
Tel: 61 1800 117 766

Massage Academy
Suite 303, 282 Victoria Avenue,
Chatswood, 2067 NSW
Tel: 61 (0)2 9410 2655

Index